Sculpture
Three dimensions in art

by Anne Civardi

HODDER
Wayland

An imprint of Hodder Headline Limited

Titles in this series:
Action! Movement in art
Families: Relationships in art
Look At Me! Self-Portraits in art
Place and Space: Landscapes in art
Sculpture: Three dimensions in art
Telling Tales: Stories in art

For more information about this series
and other Hodder Wayland titles, go to
www.hodderwayland.co.uk

Series concept: Ruth Thomson
Series Consultant: Erika Langmuir
Editor and Picture Research: Margot Richardson
Designers: Rachel Hamdi and Holly Mann

Copyright © Anne Civardi 2005

The right of Anne Civardi to be identified as the author of this
Work has been asserted by her in accordance with the
Copyright, Designs and Patents Act 1988.

British Library Cataloguing in Publication Data
  Civardi, Anne
  Sculpture secrets. - (Artventure)
  1.Sculpture - Juvenile literature 2.Art appreciation -
  Juvenile literature
  I.Title
  730.1'17

  ISBN 0 7502 45735

The publishers would like to thank the following for permission
to reproduce their pictures:
Page 1 © Massimo Listri/CORBIS; page 4 photos © Anne Civardi;
page 5 © Barry Flanagan/Collection Walker Art Center:
Minneapolis. Gift of Anne Larsen Simonson and Glen and
Marilyn Nelson, 1987; page 6 © Brooklyn Museum of
Art/CORBIS; page 7 © Massimo Listri/CORBIS; page 8
© Wolfgang Kaehler/CORBIS; page 9 (top) Tomb of Qin shi
Huang Di, Xianyang, China/www.bridgeman.co.uk; page 9
(bottom) © Wolfgang Kaehler/CORBIS; pages 10-11
© The George and Helen Segal Foundation, DACS
London/VAGA, New York 2004 / National Gallery of Canada;
pages 12-13 The works illustrated have been reproduced by
permission of the Henry Moore Foundation / photography by
[p.12 left] Michel Muller, [p.12 right] Georgina Gauntlett and
[p.3] Michael Phipps; page 14 Museo dell'Opera del Duomo,
Florence, Italy/www.bridgeman.co.uk; page 15 British Museum;
page 16 © Archivo Iconografico, S.A./CORBIS; page 17 ©
Bowness, Hepworth Estate/National Museum of Women in the
Arts, Washington DC (Gift of Wallace and Wilhelmina Holladay);
page 18 © AGDAP Paris and DACS London 2004 / Robert
Harding World Imagery; page 19 © ADAGP, Paris and DACS,
London 2004 / Julia Waterlow; Eye Ubiquitous/CORBIS; page 20
© Claes Oldenburg and Coosje van Bruggen/Art Gallery of
Ontario, Toronto (Purchase, 1967); page 21 © Claes Oldenburg
and Coosje van Bruggen/Collection Walker Art Center,
Minneapolis. Gift of Frederick R. Weisman in honor of his
parents, William and Mary Weisman, 1988; page 22 Staatliche
Kunstsammlungen, Dresden; 23 © Madame Tussauds, London;
24 © Deborah Butterfield/photo courtesy of Arizona State
University Art Museum, Tempe, Arizona, USA; 25 © ADAGP,
Paris and DACS, London 2004/Hirshhorn Museum and Sculpture
Garden, Smithsonian Institution, (Gift of Mary and Leigh B.
Block, by exchange, 1989), photo by Lee Stalsworth; 26 © Andy
Goldsworthy; 27 © Andy Goldsworthy/photo courtesy of Stanford
University News Service Library, Stanford, California.

weblinks

For more information about
three dimensions in art, go to
www.waylinks.co.uk/series/
artventure/sculpture

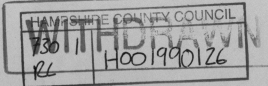

Contents

All sorts of sculpture   4

Spectacular stone   6

Clever clay   8

Perfect plaster   10

Brilliant bronze   12

Wonderful wood   14

Marble magic   16

Painted polyester   18

From soft to steel sculpture   20

Wild wax   22

Fantastic found objects   24

Back to nature   26

About the artists   28

Glossary   31

Index   32

Words in **bold** can be found in the glossary

All sorts of sculpture

Sculptures are works of art that, unlike paintings, drawings or prints, are made in three dimensions: height, width and depth. Some are life-like, while others are just simple shapes and forms.

A mass of materials

Sculptors use all sorts of materials, such as clay, **plaster**, wood, **bronze** and other **metals**, plastic or wax, and even chocolate or ice.

They may choose a material because it lasts for a long time and stands up to all kinds of weather. They may use it to convey an idea or feeling about the sculpture, or to give it a particular character or **texture**.

◀ This **clay** dog is about 2,000 years old. It was made by the Colima Indians of Mexico. Although this statue is quite small, some statues of Colima dogs were made bigger than life-size.

▶ Before the clay was baked hard, it was painted reddish-brown and then burnished, or polished, with a stone to give it a shiny finish.

- Do you think this dog looks life-like?
- What makes it look different from the dogs you see today?
- Do you think the dog looks fierce or friendly?
- Notice the different colours of the baked clay.

◀ Sculptures like this one were often found in graves. They were thought to lead the dead person's spirit into the next world.

❑ Unkown artist
Colima Dog
about 100BC-AD250

Creating colours

Although both the hare and the bell of this sculpture by Barry Flanagan, a British sculptor, were cast in bronze, the surfaces are different colours. Sculptors can create the colours, or **patinas**, they want (see page 13). Sometimes bronze or copper turns greeny-blue when it is very old and weathered.

◀ Look at how Flanagan has managed to make the leaping hare look so playful, while the huge, elegant bell gives a feeling of strength and stability.

❏ Barry Flanagan
Hare on Bell on Portland Stone Piers
1983

Modelled, carved or constructed?

Some sculptures are created by modelling soft materials, such as clay or plaster. Others are made by **carving** away materials, such as wood or stone. Sculptures may also be constructed, or assembled, from objects, such as metal, wood, old tyres or wire.

• Why do you think the sculptor has included the stone blocks the sculpture is resting on?

• Look at how Flanagan has managed to give the hare a sense of movement.

Spectacular stone

Stone carving dates back over 26,000 years and is one of the oldest surviving forms of art. Most stone is hard and can be difficult to carve, but it lasts for a very long time.

What a relief!

This raised carved picture, created over 2,700 years ago, is called a **relief**. It was made to decorate the **tomb** of Iuput II, an Egyptian Pharaoh.

Egyptian art

The Ancient Egyptians believed that if a relief, statue or even a painting looked like the person it represented, it would help his or her soul to live forever. Egyptian sculpture followed a certain style so that it was as easy to understand as possible. In reliefs or paintings, the head of a figure was always shown sideways, in **profile**. The eye and the top half of the body was seen from the front, while the legs were turned to the same side as the head, with one foot placed in front of the other.

❏ Unknown artist
Egyptian Plaque of Iuput II
about 750–710BC

Think about the texture of these two sculptures.

• Do you think they would be hard or soft, smooth or bumpy?

• Notice how delicately the face and the clothes of the pharaoh have been carved, as well as the hair and the necklace.

□ Giovanni da Bologna (also called Giambologna)
Giant Statue of the Apennine
1569-81

Colossal creation

Giambologna, a Flemish-Italian sculptor working in the sixteenth century, created this giant statue (13.8 metres high) more than 430 years ago. Carved from an enormous block of **limestone**, it sits perched on a rock in a garden near Florence in Italy.

Before the sculptor started carving, the block was split into roughly the right shape. Giambologna probably drew the outline of the figure on to the stone. Then he chipped away with his **chisels** and **mallet** until the figure emerged. It took him almost twelve years to finish.

There is a big cave, or grotto, at the base of the figure, and a room in his huge head.

Clever clay

For thousands of years, people have **modelled** sculptures out of clay, a kind of earth that can be moulded or sculpted easily when it is wet, but hardens when it dries.

Underground army

These clay soldiers and the horses opposite were created over 2,200 years ago to guard the body of the first Emperor of China, Qin Shi Huang Di, inside his tomb. They are made of **terracotta**, a reddish-brown clay that has been baked, or fired, in an especially hot oven, called a kiln. This makes it hard and stops it from crumbling. Fired clay can last almost as long as stone, although it breaks more easily.

❏ Unknown artists
Terracotta Soldiers from the Tomb of Qin Shi Huang Di
about 211-206BC
These are just a few of the underground soldiers buried in the tomb. Emperor Qin Shi Huang Di ordered them to be created to defend him, and to make sure he remained safe and powerful after he had died.

Terracotta troops

The warriors were discovered in 1974 by three farmers while they were digging a well. When archaeologists excavated the area, they found more than 8,000 life-sized, painted terracotta soldiers and horses, arranged in battle formation. Each soldier was different from the others, with a different head-dress, costume, face and even moustache.

❑ Unknown artists
Terracotta Horses and Chariot from the Tomb of Qin Shi Huang Di

When the the tomb, which took over thirty-five years to create, was finished, the Emperor and all his treasures were buried deep under the ground. Before the workers who constructed the tomb could leave, it was sealed, trapping them inside forever.

Softly does it

The terracotta figures and horses were modelled in clay while it was still soft. Before the clay hardened, the sculptures were hollowed out. This allowed moisture to escape when they were baked in the kiln. Otherwise steam pressure would have made them blow up.

❑ Unknown artists
Terracotta Soldiers from the Tomb of Qin Shi Huang Di

Look closely at the terracotta soldiers on the left and far left.
- How many different moustaches can you spot?
- How many different head-dresses can you see?
- Look at the soldiers that have lost their heads. Notice how they have been hollowed out.

Perfect plaster

Some sculptors use plaster, a mixture of sand and lime, to create their works of art. Plaster can be modelled by mixing it with water, or carved from a solid block. It is also used to make a **cast** (see page 12).

❏ George Segal
The Gas Station (detail)
1963

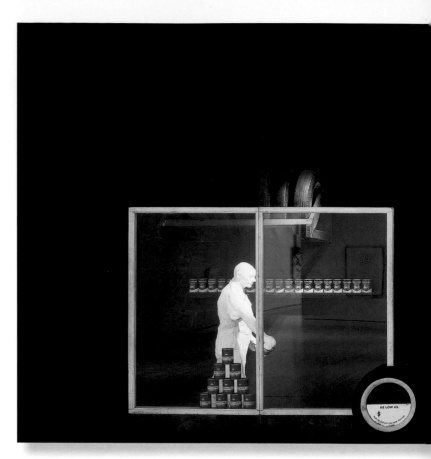

An artist's aim

George Segal, a **contemporary** American sculptor, is famous for his life-sized, plaster figures. He was most interested in creating sculptures showing ordinary people doing everyday things, such as waiting for a bus or listening to the radio. He wanted his sculptures to remind people of what it is like to be human.

Plaster people

To make each of the figures in the sculpture above, Segal wrapped bandages around the body of a model who adopted the pose Segal chose. Then he covered the bandages with wet plaster.

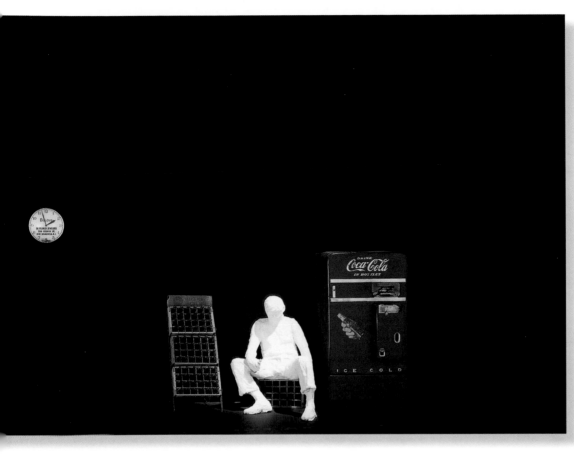

□ George Segal
The Gas Station
1963
This sculpture includes a red Coca-Cola machine, 71 glass bottles, 4 wooden crates, 8 rubber tyres, a tyre rack, 30 oil cans, an electric clock, 6 concrete blocks and 2 windows of wood and plate glass.

When the plaster had dried, he carefully cut it off the model in sections. Then he joined the pieces together to form a hollow plaster figure. Finally, he placed the figures in a sculpted scene that resembled a petrol station (known as a gas station in the USA).

Plaster people

The sculptor used models, mostly his family and friends, who were sensitive to his feelings and whose personalities he could capture in his pieces. He said about this sculpture: 'I am interested in the colours, the lights, the tired young man, the energetic older man and how long it takes me to walk the long corridor.'

- How would you describe the mood of the younger man (sitting down)?
- Why do you think Segal has included the clock floating in the middle of the piece?
- Why do you think Segal has used such a dark background colour?

Brilliant bronze

Many famous sculptors have created huge sculptures cast from bronze and other metals.

Mini maquettes

To create this sculpture of a mother and child, Henry Moore, a twentieth-century British sculptor, first made a small three-dimensional plaster model, called a **maquette** (pictured below). By making the maquette, Moore could study the form in his hand, understand its shape from all round, and see what the finished sculpture would look like.

❏ Henry Moore
Full-size plaster cast of **Draped Reclining Mother and Baby**
1983 (LH822)

❏ Henry Moore
Maquette for Draped Reclining Mother and Baby
1981 (LH820) plaster

Working model

The artist then made a larger plaster working model, about three times the size of his maquette.

Polystyrene and plaster

The next stage was to enlarge the plaster working model, again by about three times the size, but this time in polystyrene, a material that is light and quick to work with. As it is not possible to create any detail on the surface of polystyrene, a plaster cast (pictured above) was made from it. The artist then worked on the full-sized plaster cast, altering some parts as well as adding texture.

- Look at all the different shapes, curves and hollows Moore has included in his piece.
- Does this sculpture look realistic or not to you?
- Notice how the texture on the bronze figures helps to give shadows and definition.

❏ Henry Moore
Final bronze of **Draped Reclining Mother and Baby**
1983 (LH 822)
Henry Moore's work was often based on the human figure. He created many sculptures of one of his favourite themes, mother and child. He was 85 years old when he finished this sculpture. It combines three of his favourite themes: mother and child; reclining figure; and an outer form shielding an inner form, the mother protecting her baby.

Fantastic foundry

When Moore was satisfied that it was ready to be cast in bronze, the huge plaster model was sent to a special workshop called a **foundry**. Here the sculpture was cast in several pieces which were then **welded** together. To take out the welding marks, the bronze, which looked dull when it had been cast, was buffed up and polished using a sanding machine.

Moore then applied chemicals to the surface that reacted with the bronze to create a coloured patina, usually gold, brown or green. Finally the sculpture was protected by coating it with beeswax.

Wonderful wood

Sculptures can be carved out of different kinds of wood. Some hardwoods, such as beech, ash and cherry, can be polished until they shine. Softwoods, such as pine and spruce, are easier to carve, but do not polish up as well.

Mary Magdalene

The Italian sculptor, Donatello, created the painted wooden sculpture opposite in the fifteenth century. It shows Mary Magdalene, one of Jesus's followers, praying in the desert where she had gone to live after Jesus was killed on the cross.

Even though he was seventy years old when he sculpted her, Donatello has managed to capture Mary's sad, tormented expression and her long bedraggled hair, as well as the folds of the ragged dress hanging off her thin body. He was able to carve such realistic figures because of his great knowledge of the human body.

- Which foot do you think Mary Magdalene is putting her weight on to?
- How do you think the woman is feeling?
- Do you think this woman is young or old? Notice her neck and the veins on her feet.

❏ Donatello
Mary Magdalene, *1454-55*

Clever chiselers

Some sculptors use knives to whittle or carve wood. Others use different shaped metal chisels and a mallet. In many parts of Africa, sculptors use a tool called an adze, which has a sharp, curved blade.

Making faces

This carved wooden dance mask seems to combine both human and animal features. Although it is far less realistic and detailed than Donatello's sculpture, it is still very striking. The African sculptor has used strong lines and simple shapes to create the long, smooth forehead, tiny ears, cone-shaped nose and small, round mouth. In profile, the curved line that joins the forehead to the nose makes a delicate 'S' shape.

Working in wood

Wood has always been the most important material used for sculpture in Africa. African sculptures have inspired the work of many modern artists, such as Pablo Picasso and Constantin Brancusi.

• Look at the curved shapes of the face: the chin, the line of the beard that joins the hair, and the eyebrows.

• What other shapes can you see?

• What animal does the mask remind you of?

❑ Unknown artist, Guro people
Dance Mask
19th Century
Carved by the Guro people of the Ivory Coast in West Africa, this dance mask was probably used in celebrations and ceremonies.

15

Marble magic

Although **marble** is a very hard stone and difficult to carve, many famous sculptors have turned huge blocks of it into magnificent, life-like works of art. Marble comes in many beautiful colours and can be polished to a dazzling shine.

A marble tree

Bernini, a seventeenth-century Italian sculptor, carved this white marble statue when he was only twenty-four years old. It shows the moment in a Greek **myth** when Apollo, the god of the sun, catches up with a beautiful **nymph** named Daphne, with whom he has fallen in love. Daphne begs her father, a river god, to help her escape Apollo's grasp, and he immediately turns her into a laurel tree.

- Look at the leaves sprouting from Daphne's fingers. What other parts of her body are turning into a tree?
- How can you tell that Apollo has been running?
- Describe the look on Daphne's face.
- How do you think Apollo is feeling? Describe the look on his face.

❑ Gian Lorenzo Bernini
Apollo and Daphne
1622-25

Careful carvers

Sculptors have to be very careful when they carve stone or wood. If they make a mistake, or carve off a piece they do not intend, they cannot replace it.

By using different chisels or **rasps**, they can give the surface of stone a certain feel or texture. Some tools create marks, grooves or ridges, while others can be used to make the stone rough or smooth.

Abstract art

Not all sculptors create pieces that look like real people, animals or objects. The twentieth-century British artist, Barbara Hepworth, preferred to carve **abstract** pieces. She has focused on lines, shapes and material rather than any recognizable or realistic form.

Although this sculpture is not realistic, it is still based on the female form. Hepworth has used the central hole to great effect, with the soft, curving shapes surrounding it representing the shape of a woman's body.

Hepworth was the first person to carve holes *through* her pieces, and became famous for this style of sculpture.

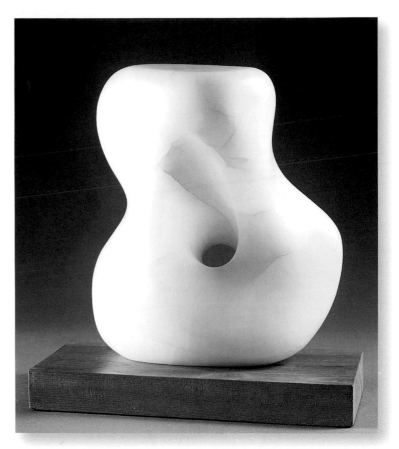

❏ Barbara Hepworth
Merryn
1962

- If you could name the piece yourself, what would you call it?
- Which parts of the sculpture look like a woman's body?
- Notice where the shadows fall and how they help to give the sculpture form.
- What is the base the sculpture is resting on made of?

Painted polyester

Sculptures can be cast in **polyester**, a material used to make plastic.
When it has been cast, the sculpture is hollow and strong.

❑ Niki de Saint Phalle
Firebird
(Stravinsky Fountain)
1983

Colourful creations

Niki de Saint Phalle, a French sculptor, is most famous for her huge, dazzlingly-coloured figures. Her early sculptures were made from papier mâché (paper and glue) over chicken wire frames. In 1964 she started using polyester. This allowed her to produce sculptures in her own style with soft, curvy lines. It also made it possible for her to work on big, painted, outdoor sculptures which were waterproof, sturdy and did not rust.

The sculptor believed in the freedom of spirit and created her works by following her emotions. She once said: 'I was doing as I always did. I don't think when I work. I feel. I work by instinct. I work by what I have to do.'

Look at all the different colours the sculptor has used.
- How many can you spot?
- What colour jumps out?
- How do the colours make you feel?
- Notice how big the sculpture is by looking at the size of the people around it.

❏ Niki de Saint Phalle
Elephant (Stravinsky Fountain)
1983

Inspired by music

Together with her husband, Jean Tinguely (another famous sculptor), Niki made sixteen different sculptures for a fountain close to the Pompidou Centre, in Paris, France. The sculptures, which squirt jets of water, were inspired by a piece of music, called *Firebird*, created by the composer Ivor Stravinsky. The colourful elephant sculpture pictured above is also part of the Stravinsky fountain.

While Niki's pieces are brightly-painted, magical, playful figures, Tinguely's are more mechanical, constructed from wheels, motors, iron and other machine parts. You can see one of his pieces beside Niki's *Firebird* sculpture *(left)*.

From soft to steel sculpture

Artists can use almost any material to create sculptures. Claes Oldenburg, an American, is famous for his soft sculptures, which he made out of **canvas**, plastic or **vinyl**. He also uses hard materials, such as steel.

He created sculptures of everyday things people might find at home, such as a clothes peg, a tube of toothpaste, a Swiss army knife a toaster, a hamburger and even a cherry balancing on a spoon.

❏ Claes Oldenburg
Floor Burger
1962

- How many layers is this sculpture made up of?
- Does this hamburger look real to you? Which part looks the most realistic?
- What type of food do you think is resting on the top of the sculpture?

Chicago creations

Oldenburg was inspired by objects he saw lying on the streets of Chicago, where he lived as a child. He once said: 'The street, in particular, fascinated me. I discovered a whole world of objects I had never known before. Ordinary packages became sculpture in my eye.'

Huge hamburger

All of the sculptor's creations are much bigger than life. The soft sculpture of the hamburger above, made from painted canvas and filled with foam rubber, is as big as a bed. He has also made a 3.75 m long sculpture of an icecream, a baked potato as big as a car and a 13.5 m high clothes peg.

Cherry on a spoon

Claes Oldenburg liked to make sculptures that reminded him of something. The spoon of this huge painted steel and aluminium piece reminded him of a **Viking** boat with its prow out of the water. His wife, Coosje van Bruggen, who thought up the idea of the cherry, helped him design the sculpture. The sculpture is one of two fountain sculptures Oldenburg created with his wife. It is obvious from his pieces that the sculptor had a good sense of humour.

- What is the first thing that catches your eye in this sculpture? Why?
- Notice how the huge cherry is balancing on the spoon. How do you think it stays there?
- Look at the top of the cherry's stalk. This is where the water squirts out of the fountain.

21

Wild wax

Although the sculptures on these two pages look quite different from each other, they are both modelled in wax.

Modern sculpture

Medardo Rosso, a nineteenth-century Italian sculptor, created the head *(right)*. One of the founders of modern sculpture, he preferred to create art of things that captured a moment in everyday life, such as a woman laughing or a child crying.

After experimenting with different materials, Rosso concentrated on modelling with wax over plaster. This allowed him to capture the light, mood, atmosphere and feelings of his subjects.

- What emotion has Rosso managed to capture on the child's face?
- What effect does the darker colour of the wax have on the sculpture?

❑ Medardo Rosso, **Bambino Malato (ill child)**, *1893*

Just a suggestion

Instead of modelling detailed faces, Rosso gave only a suggestion of a person's features. The fragile face of the sick child above is full of quiet emotion and pain, with the head tilted to one side, the eyes closed and the mouth barely open. It almost has the quality of a blurred or damaged photograph.

Tussaud talent

This sculpture of Kylie Minogue was created for Madame Tussauds in London, England, along with 200 other figures of famous celebrities and historical figures.

Madame Tussaud, a talented sculptor in the eighteeth century, was taught wax modelling by a doctor for whom she worked. During the French Revolution, she was forced to make hundreds of wax death masks of victims beheaded at the guillotine.

Although Madame Tussaud died in 1850, her collection gradually grew into the world famous attraction that bears her name.

- Look at how realistically the figure has been painted: the colour of the skin, the eyes, the lipstick and the bright red nail varnish.
- Do you think this sculpture looks like Kylie Minogue?

❑ **Kylie Minogue figure**, *2002*

Working with wax

The sculpture was first modelled in clay around a steel and aluminium framework, called an **armature**. The head and hands were cast in beeswax coloured with oil paints to give a realistic skin tone, but the body was cast in **resin** and **fibreglass** to make it extra strong. The hair, which is real hair, and the eyebrows, were punched into the wax strand by strand. When all the body parts had been carefully fitted together, the figure was dressed in copies of clothes and jewellery Kylie had once worn herself.

Fantastic found objects

For over 100 years, sculptors have used objects they find around them (found objects) to construct their works of art. These objects may be natural (wood, stone, vines, plants, flowers) or **manufactured** (cloth, paper, metal and even old tyres).

❏ Deborah Butterfield
Horse # 2-85
1985
Deborah Butterfield has loved horses since she was a child. She lives and works on a ranch in Montana, USA, where she looks after several of her own horses. These horses are the inspiration for many of her sculptures.

Horse creations

For the past twenty years, Deborah Butterfield, an American, has concentrated on creating sculptures of horses. Although the one above is constructed from pieces of broken wood and twisted, rusty metal, the artist has still managed to capture the spirit, beauty and mood of the horse.

The sculptor chooses her materials very carefully and tries to alter their shape and colour as little as possible.

- How do you think this horse is feeling?
- Look at how Butterfield has suggested the horse's strong neck and shoulders.
- What found materials or objects is this horse made from?

Horse talk

Butterfield sees her horse sculptures as a way to communicate and identify with these powerful creatures that have played such a important role in human civilization.

Dubuffet was not interested in creating beautiful sculptures. Instead, he tried to give them a rough, raw, earthy look by keeping the **organic** materials in their original state.

- If you could name this sculpture, what would you call it?
- Can you see the face, the arms and the legs of the grapevine figure?

◀ The sculpture is mounted on a **slag** base, with tar, rope, wire, twine and nails.

❏ Jean Dubuffet
The Soul of Morvan
1954

This sculpture represents a gnarled, weather-worn old man working in a vineyard. To construct it, Jean Dubuffet, a French artist who worked in the twentieth century, used grapevines from the wine-growing region of Morvan, in France.

Back to nature

All around the world, there are sculptors who work with whatever they can find around them in nature: sticks, twigs, leaves, feathers, shells, bones, pebbles, sand, and even ice and snow.

Not made to last

Andy Goldsworthy, a British sculptor, creates natural pieces, most of which only last for a moment or a few hours. This ice spiral, formed from icicles frozen together around a tree trunk, melted soon after it was made. A tower of stones the sculptor built on the sea shore at low tide toppled over as soon as the water swirled in. Before each piece disappears, Goldsworthy captures it in a photograph.

The sculptor once said: 'I enjoy the freedom of just using my hands and *found* tools – a sharp stone, the quill of a feather, thorns. I take the opportunities each day offers: if it is snowing, I work with snow; at leaf-fall, it will be with leaves.'

- How many times does the spiral twist around the tree?
- Look at how thin the icicles become the higher up the tree trunk they twist and curl.

❏ Andy Goldsworthy
Ice Spiral
1984

26

River of stone

This more permanent sculpture by Andy Goldsworthy is set in the grounds of Stanford University, California, USA. It was created from 6,500 stones taken from buildings that collapsed on campus during the 1906 and 1989 Californian earthquakes.

When the sculptor found out about the stone, he said: 'The idea of stone that was once a building returned to the ground, back into the earth, for a work that is about flow, movement and change, it was perfect. It was really perfect.'

Goldsworthy was excited by the clear, bright, intense light of Northern California and the way it seemed to change the look of his sculpture at different times of the day. He said that his sculpture was as much about light as stone.

❏ Andy Goldsworthy
Stone River
1993

About the artists

The symbols below show the size and shape of the works shown in this book, compared with an average-sized adult.

Gian Lorenzo BERNINI (page 16)

(1598-1680) Italian (Naples)
Apollo and Daphne, 1622-25
Marble, 243 cm high
Galleria Borghese, Rome, Italy

Other works

❏ *Boy with a Dragon*, 1614-20
   J Paul Getty Museum, Los Angeles, CA, USA
❏ *Pluto and Proserpina*, 1621-22
   Galleria Borghese, Rome, Italy
❏ *Louis XIV*, 1665, Château de Versailles, France

Deborah BUTTERFIELD (page 24)

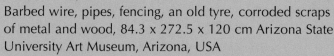

(1949-) American (San Diego)
Horse #2-85, 1985
Barbed wire, pipes, fencing, an old tyre, corroded scraps of metal and wood, 84.3 x 272.5 x 120 cm Arizona State University Art Museum, Arizona, USA

Other works

❏ *Nahele*, 1986
   The Contemporay Museum, Honolulu, Hawaii, USA
❏ *Rex*, 1991
   Lowe Art Museum, University of Miami, Florida, USA
❏ *Aluminum Horse*, 1982
   San Diego Museum of Art, San Diego, CA, USA

DONATELLO (page 14)

(about 1386-1466) Italian (Florence)
Mary Magdalene, about 1454-55
Wood with polychromy and gold, 188 cm high
Museo dell'Opera del Duomo, Florence, Italy

Other works

❏ *Saint John the Baptist*, 1438
   Santa Maria Gloriosa dei Frari, Venice, Italy
❏ *Crucifix*, 1412-13
   Santa Croce, Florence, Italy

Jean DUBUFFET (page 25)

(1901-85) French (Le Havre)
The Soul of Morvan, 1954
Grape wood and vines mounted on slag base, with tar, rope, wire, twine, nails and staples
46.5 x 38.9 x 32.4 cm
Hirshhorn Museum and Sculpture Garden, Washington DC, USA

Other works

❏ *The Inquisitor*, 1973
   Museum of Fine Arts, Boston, MASS, USA
❏ *Groupe de Quatre Arbres*, 1972
   Chase Manhattan Bank, New York, NY, USA

Barry FLANAGAN (page 5)

(1941-) British (Prestatyn)
Hare on Bell on Portland Stone Piers, 1983
Bronze and limestone
259 x 284.5 x 190.5 cm
Collection Walker Art Center, Minneapolis, USA
Gift of Anne Larsen Simonson and Glen and Marilyn Nelson, 1987

Other works

❏ *Nijinski Hare*, 1996
   Waddington Galleries, London, UK
❏ *Thinker on Rock*, 1997
   Waddington Galleries, London, UK
❏ *30ft Acrobats*, 2000
   New Art Centre Sculpture Park and Gallery, Roche Court, Wiltshire, UK

Jean Boulogne GIAMBOLOGNA (Giovanni da Bologna) (pages 1, 7)

(1529-1608) Flemish (Douai)
Giant Statue of the Apennine, 1569-81
Limestone, 13.8 metres high
Garden of the Villa Demidoff,
Pratolino, Florence, Italy

Other works
❑ *Ferdinand Ler*, 1594, Louvre, Paris, France
❑ *Fountain of Venus*, c.1575
   Garden of Boboli, Florence, Italy
❑ *Virtue Defeating Vice*, 1565
   National Museum of Bargello, Florence, Italy

Andy GOLDSWORTHY (pages 26-27)

(1956-) British (Cheshire)
Ice Spiral, 1984
Individual icicles joined together to form a spiral
Stone River, 1993
Sandstone, 105 cm high x 120 cm wide x 98.5 m long
Stanford University Museum of Art, Stanford, California, USA

Other works
❑ *Three Cairns*, 2002, Des Moines Art Centre, Iowa, USA
❑ *Pebbles around a Hole*, 1987, Kiinagashima-cho, Japan
❑ *Rowan Leaves with Hole*, 1987
   Yorkshire Sculpture Park, West Bretton, Wakefield, UK

Barbara HEPWORTH (page 17)

(1903-75) British (Wakefield, Yorkshire)
Merryn, 1962
Alabaster with wood, 32.5 x 28.75 x 20.6 cm
The National Museum of Women in the Arts,
Washington DC, USA

Other works
❑ *Figure, 1933*, 1933, Tate Liverpool, UK
❑ *Sculpture with Profiles*, 1932
   Barbara Hepworth Museum and Sculpture
   Garden, St Ives, Cornwall, UK
❑ *Untitled*, 1960
   University of Lethbridge, Alberta, Canada

Henry MOORE (pages 12-13)

(1898-1986) British (Castleford)
*Draped Reclining Mother
and Baby*, 1983, Bronze, 265.5 cm long
The Henry Moore Foundation, Perry Green, Herts, UK

Other works
❑ *Family Group*, about 1944
   Ball State Museum of Art, Indiana, IN, USA
❑ *Draped Reclining Figure*, 1952-53
   Hirshhorn Museum and Sculpture Garden,
   Washington DC, USA
❑ *Reclining Figure*, 1938
   Peggy Guggenheim Collection, Venice, Italy

Claes OLDENBURG (page 20)

(1912-) Swedish (Stockholm)
Floor Burger, 1962
Painted canvas and foam rubber,
132.1 cm high x 213.4 cm wide
Art Gallery of Ontario, Canada

Other works
❑ *Floor Cake*, 1963
   Museum of Modern Art, New York, NY, USA
❑ *Soft Pay-Telephone*, 1963
   Guggenheim Museum, New York, NY, USA
❑ *7-Up*, 1961, Hirshhorn Museum and Sculpture
   Garden, Washington DC, USA
❑ *Plantoir*, 2001
   Museum of Fine Arts, Houston, Texas, TX, USA
❑ *Corridor Pin, Blue*, 1999
   Museum of Fine Arts, Houston, Texas, TX, USA

Claes OLDENBURG & Coosje van BRUGGEN (page 21)

Spoonbridge and Cherry, 1985-88
Aluminium, stainless steel and paint
899 x 1,570 x 411.5 cm
Collection Walker Art Center, Minneapolis, MN, USA
Gift of Frederick R Weisman in honor of his parents,
William and Mary Weisman, 1988

Medardo ROSSO (page 22)

(1858-1928) Italian (Milan)
Bambino Malato (Ill child), 1893
Beeswax over plaster, 20 x 15 x 25 cm
Staatliche Kunstsammlungen, Dresden, Germany

Other works
❏ *Laughing Woman*, 1890
   National Gallery of Australia, Canberra, Australia
❏ *Bimbo Malato* (Sick Boy), 1893
   Middlebury College Museum of Art, Vermont, VT, USA

Niki de SAINT PHALLE (pages 18-19)

(1930-2002) French (Neuilly-sur-Seine)
Firebird and *Elephant (Stravinsky Fountain)*, 1983
Painted polyester
Place Igor Stravinsky, Paris, France

Other works
❏ *Le Couple*, 1978
   Niki Museum, Nasu, Japan
❏ *Serpent Goddess*, 1987
   Didrichsen Art Museum, Helsinki, Finland

George SEGAL (pages 10-11)

(1924-2000) American (New York)
The Gas Station, 1963
2 plaster figures, Coca-Cola machine,
71 glass bottles, 4 wooden crates, metal stand, 8 rubber
tyres, tyre rack, 30 oil cans, electric clock, 6 concrete
blocks, 2 windows of wood and plate glass,
2.59 x 7.32 x 1.22 m
National Gallery of Canada, Ottawa, Ontario, Canada

Other works
❏ *Girl Resting*, 1970,
   Ackland Art Museum at the University of North Carolina,
   Raleigh, North Carolina, NC, USA
❏ *The Tightrope Walker*, 1969,
   Carnegie Museum of Art, Pittsburg, Pennsylvania, USA
❏ Bus Riders, 1962, Hirshhorn Museum and Sculpture
   Garden, Washington DC, USA

Madame TUSSAUDS (page 23)

Kylie Minogue figure, 2002
Wax, fibreglass, resin, hair, clothes and jewellery, life-size
Madame Tussauds, London, UK

Other works at
❏ Madame Tussauds: London, UK; Amsterdam, Holland;
   New York, USA; Las Vegas, USA; Hong Kong

Unknown artist, Colima (page 4)

Colima Dog, about 100BC-AD250
Terracotta, 11 x 9 x 18 cm
Collection of author

Other works
❏ *Dog with Human Mask*, about 100BC-AD250
   Dallas Museum of Art, Texas, TX, USA
❏ *Kneeling Female Effigy Figure*, 1st century BC
   Detroit Institute of Arts, Detroit, MI, USA

Unknown artist, Ancient Egyptian (page 6)

Egyptian Plaque of Iuput II, about 750-710BC
Limestone
The Brooklyn Museum of Art, New York, NY, USA

Other Ancient Egyptian reliefs
❏ *Relief of Akhty-hotep*, about 2,650-2,600BC
   The Brooklyn Museum of Art, New York, NY, USA
❏ *Carved Tomb Door, from the tomb of Iry and Inet at
   Saqqara*, about 2613-2494BC, British Museum, London, UK

Unknown artists, Chinese (pages 8-9)

Soldiers, Horses and Chariot, about 211-206BC,
Terracotta
Tomb of Qin Shi Huang Di, Xi'an, China

Unknown artist, Guro people (page 15)

Guro people, Ivory Coast, Africa
Dance Mask, 19th Century
Hardwood
British Museum

Glossary

Abstract Based on shape, line and form, rather than trying to look like real people, animals or objects.

Armature A frame around which a sculpture is modelled to keep it rigid, rather like a skeleton.

Bronze A hard-wearing metal that is a mixture of copper and tin.

Canvas A tough, heavy, fabric made from cotton.

Carving Cutting or shaping a hard material.

Cast The exact copy of a sculpture produced from a mould.

Chisels Metal tools with sharp blades used for carving wood or stone.

Clay A firm, fine-grained type of earth that can be modelled into different shapes when it is mixed with water.

Contemporary Belonging to, or taking place in the present; modern in style or design.

Fibreglass A plastic material made of glass fibres embedded in resin.

Foundry A special workshop where sculptors send their models to be cast in metal.

Limestone A soft stone used for carving.

Mallet A hammer, often with a heavy wooden head, used for hitting the end of a chisel when carving wood or stone.

Manufactured Made by people using machinery.

Maquette A small, three-dimensional clay, plaster or wax model.

Marble A very hard stone that can be polished until it shines.

Metals Hard substances, such as copper, bronze, tin, gold, silver, iron or steel, that can be shaped or moulded into a sculpture.

Modelled Made or shaped in three dimensions.

Myth A traditional story, often about supernatural beings or events.

Nymph A female spirit of nature in a myth.

Organic Related to or coming from living matter.

Patina The colour produced on the surface of a bronze or other metal sculpture, either by the weather, aging or with the use of chemicals.

Plaster A fine white powder made from a rock called gypsum.

Polyester A strong, waterproof material used to make plastic.

Profile An outline of something, usually a face, seen from one side.

Rasp A type of rough file with raised points used to smooth wood or stone.

Relief A method of carving or moulding where the design stands out from the surface.

Resin A man-made chemical used to make plastics.

Slag Stony waste matter separated from metals when they are extracted from rock.

Terracotta A type of reddish-brown baked clay. Terracotta means 'baked earth'.

Texture The feel or look of a surface.

Tomb A place where someone is buried, usually underground.

Viking Sailor from Denmark, Sweden and Norway during the eighth to eleventh centuries.

Vinyl A type of flexible plastic.

Welded Two metals joined together by heating them and fusing them to each other using another hot, melted metal.

Index

Numbers in **bold** show page numbers of illustrations

abstract 17, 31
armature 23, 31

beeswax 13, 23
Bernini, Gian Lorenzo 16, 28
 Apollo and Daphne **16**, 16, 28
bronze 4, 5, 12-13, 31
Butterfield, Deborah 24, 28
 Horse #2-85 **24**, 24, 28

canvas 20, 31
carving 5, 7, 31
cast 10, 12, 13, 18, 23, 31
chisel 7, 15, 17, 31
clay 4, 5, 8-9, 23, 31
contemporary 10, 31

Donatello 14, 28
 Mary Magdalene **14**, 14, 28
Dubuffet, Jean, 25, 28
 The Soul of Morvan **25**, 25, 28

feeling 4, 5, 10, 14, 16, 22, 24
fibreglass 23, 31
Flanagan, Barry 5, 28
 Hare on Bell on Portland Stone Piers **5**, 5, 28
found objects 24-5, 26
foundry 13, 31

Giambologna, Jean Boulogne (Giovanni da Bologna) 7, 29
 Giant Statue of the Apennine **1**, **7**, 7, 29
Goldsworthy, Andy 26-7, 29
 Ice Spiral **26**, 26, 29
 Stone River **27**, 27, 29

Hepworth, Barbara 17, 29
 Merryn **17**, 17, 29

limestone 7, 31

mallet 7, 15, 31
manufactured 24, 31
maquette 12, 31
marble 16-17, 31
metal 4, 5, 10, 12, 24, 31
modelled 5, 8, 10, 31
Moore, Henry 12-13, 29
 Draped Reclining Mother and Baby 12-13, **13**, 29
 plaster maquette **12**, 12
 full size plaster cast **12**, 12-13
myth 16, 31

nature 26-7
nymph 16, 31

Oldenburg, Claes 20-21, 29
 Floor Burger **20**, 20, 29
Oldenburg, Claes and van Bruggen, Coosje 21, 29
 Spoonbirdge and Cherry **21**, 21, 29
organic 25, 31

patina 5, 13, 31
plaster 4, 5, 10-11, 12, 13, 22, 31
plastic 4, 18, 20
polyester 18-19, 31
profile 6, 15, 31

rasp 17, 31
realistic 12, 14, 15, 17, 20, 23
relief 6, 31
resin 23, 31
Rosso, Medardo 22, 30
 Bambino Malato (Ill Child) **22**, 22, 30

Saint Phalle, Niki de 18-19, 30
 Firebird (Stravinsky Fountain) **18**, 18, 30
 Elephant (Stravinsky Fountain) **19**, 19, 30
Segal, George 10-11, 30
 The Gas Station **10-11**, 10-11, 30
slag 25, 31
steel 20-21, 23
stone 4, 5, 6-7, 8, 16, 17, 24, 26, 27

terracotta 8, 9, 30, 31
texture 4, 6, 12, 17, 31
Tinguely, Jean, 19
tomb 6, 8, 9, 31

Tussauds, Madame 23, 30
 Kylie Minogue figure **23**, 23, 30

Unknown artist, Colima 4, 30
 Colima dog **4**, 4, 30
Unknown artist, Ancient Egyptian 6, 30
 Egyptian Plaque of Iuput II, **6**, 6, 30
Unknown artist, Chinese 8-9, 30
 Soldiers, Horses and Chariot **8-9**, 8-9, 30
Unknown artist, Guro people 15, 30
 Dance Mask **15**, 15, 30

Viking 21, 31
vinyl 20, 31

wax 4, 22-3
welded 13, 31
wood 4, 5, 11, 14-15, 17, 24